The Complete Book Of Peruvian Knowledge:
Since Before the Beginning of Time!

By
Mel Waller

Life Transformation Publishing
All Rights Reserved 2020

ISBN: 9798550080702

Life Transformation Publishing
www.lifetransformationpublishing.com
melwaller@gmail.com
(email is the best way to reach us)

Specializing in Transforming Lives!

CONTENTS

Introduction   4

Conclusion   102

INTRODUCTION

Following years of extensive research with the best and brightest minds that Peru has to offer, we have compiled this exhaustive and complete treasure house of all the available Peruvian knowledge.

We hope this meets with your satisfaction!

Mel Waller

DEDICATION

This Book is hereby dedicated to Joseph Rebisz!

Joe, you know you were very instrumental for this project to become a reality and for that, I am deeply grateful. Thank You!!!

Mel Waller

Lo que sea!

Lo que sea!

Lo que sea!

Lo que sea!

Lo que sea!

Lo que sea!

Lo que sea!

Lo que sea!

Lo que sea!

Lo que sea!

Lo que sea!

Lo que sea!

Lo que sea!

Lo que sea!

Lo que sea!

Lo que sea!

Lo que sea!

Lo que sea!

Lo que sea!

Lo que sea!

Lo que sea!

Lo que sea!

Lo que sea!

Lo que sea!

Lo que sea!

Lo que sea!

Lo que sea!

Lo que sea!

Lo que sea!

Lo que sea!

Lo que sea!

Lo que sea!

Lo que sea!

Lo que sea!

Lo que sea!

Lo que sea!

Lo que sea!

Lo que sea!

Lo que sea!

Lo que sea!

Lo que sea!

Lo que sea!

Lo que sea!

Lo que sea!

Lo que sea!

Lo que sea!

Lo que sea!

Lo que sea!

Lo que sea!

Lo que sea!

Lo que sea!

Lo que sea!

Lo que sea!

Lo que sea!

Lo que sea!

59

Lo que sea!

Lo que sea!

Lo que sea!

Lo que sea!

Lo que sea!

Lo que sea!

65

Lo que sea!

Lo que sea!

Lo que sea!

Lo que sea!

Lo que sea!

Lo que sea!

Lo que sea!

Lo que sea!

Lo que sea!

Lo que sea!

75

Lo que sea!

Lo que sea!

Lo que sea!

Lo que sea!

Lo que sea!

Lo que sea!

Lo que sea!

Lo que sea!

Lo que sea!

Lo que sea!

Lo que sea!

Lo que sea!

Lo que sea!

Lo que sea!

Lo que sea!

Lo que sea!

Lo que sea!

Lo que sea!

Lo que sea!

Lo que sea!

Lo que sea!

Lo que sea!

Lo que sea!

Lo que sea!

Lo que sea!

Lo que sea!

Conclusion

We truly hope you got a good laugh from this book.

I'm American, but am 50% Norwegian on my Father's side and we used to joke about this regarding Norwegians when he was alive.

That inspired me to do other books for other people.

Love You Dad!

www.ingramcontent.com/pod-product-compliance
Lightning Source LLC
Chambersburg PA
CBHW022205150726
47992CB00002B/958